333 WORD BOOK™

WORLD at WORK

Illustrated by Robert Durham

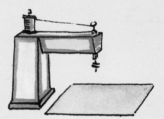

DERRYDALE BOOKS
New York

IN A TOY FACTORY

timecards

lunch box

dollhouse

toy duck

time clock

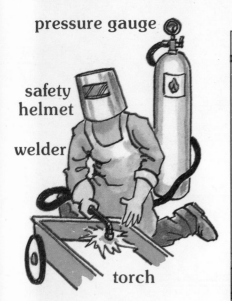

pressure gauge

safety helmet

welder

torch

stapler

robot

industrial vacuum cleaner

scissors

packing material

awl

hand truck

teddy bear

sprinkler

extension cord

soccer ball

exit sign

toy truck

jack-in-the-box

thread

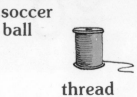

sewing machine

coffee maker

styrofoam cups

fluorescent light

fan

freight elevator

compressor

spray gun

apron

grease gun

building blocks

rocking horse

supervisor

clipboard

refrigerator

conveyor belt

wagon

AT A SERVICE STATION

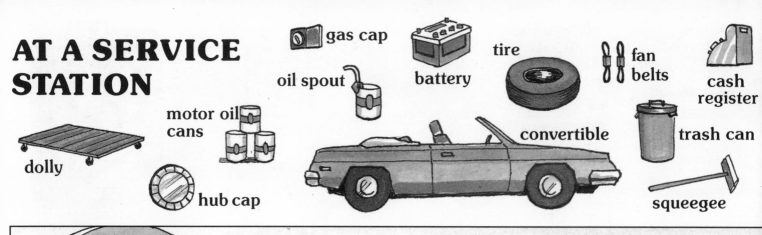

gas cap

oil spout

battery

tire

fan belts

cash register

motor oil cans

convertible

trash can

dolly

hub cap

squeegee

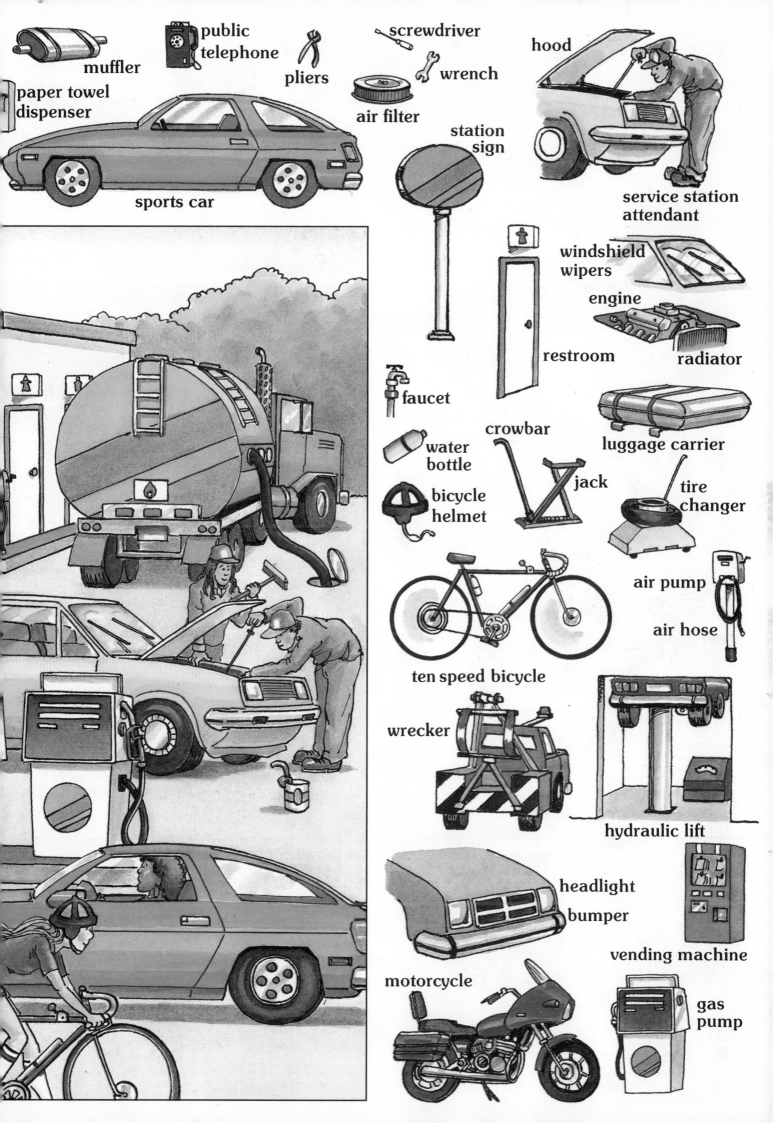

muffler

public telephone

screwdriver

wrench

hood

pliers

paper towel dispenser

air filter

sports car

station sign

service station attendant

windshield wipers

engine

restroom

radiator

faucet

crowbar

luggage carrier

water bottle

jack

tire changer

bicycle helmet

air pump

air hose

ten speed bicycle

wrecker

hydraulic lift

headlight

bumper

vending machine

motorcycle

gas pump

AT THE AIRPORT

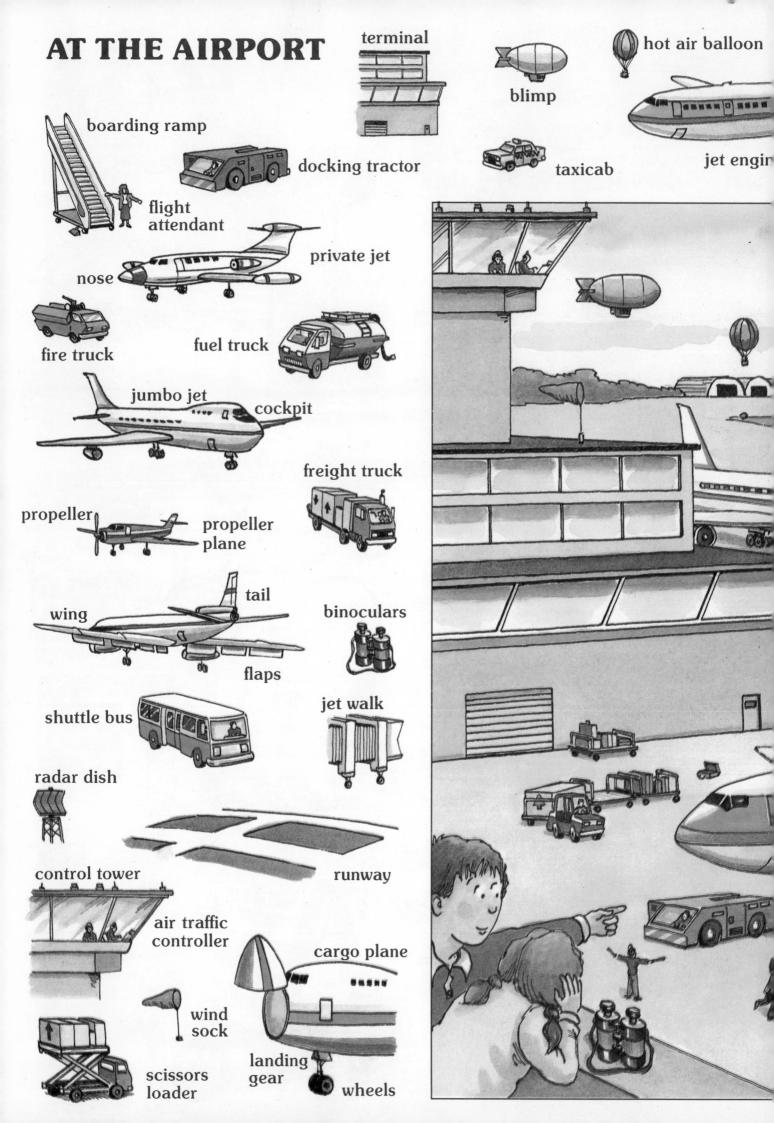

terminal

blimp

hot air balloon

boarding ramp

docking tractor

taxicab

jet engine

flight attendant

private jet

nose

fire truck

fuel truck

jumbo jet

cockpit

freight truck

propeller

propeller plane

wing

tail

binoculars

flaps

shuttle bus

jet walk

radar dish

control tower

runway

air traffic controller

cargo plane

wind sock

scissors loader

landing gear

wheels

jetliner

rudder

helicopter

rotors

docking director

baggage cart

passenger

ambulance

landing pad

generator

hangars

ON THE RAILROAD

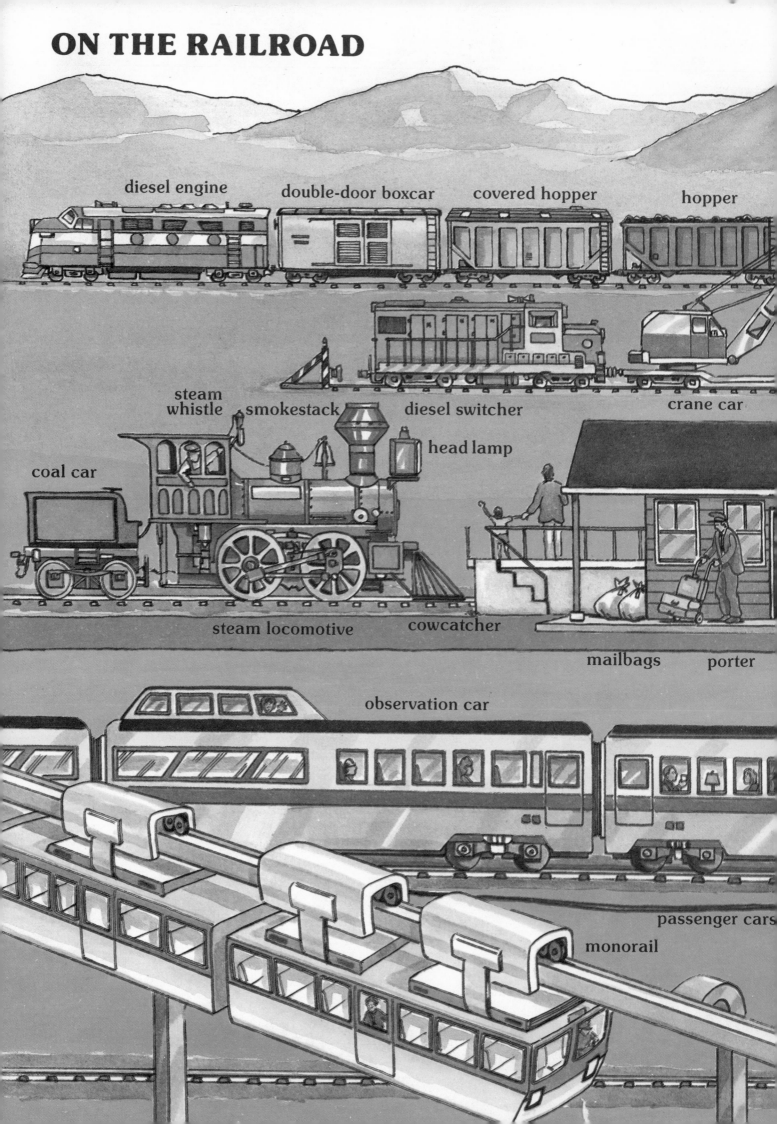

diesel engine

double-door boxcar

covered hopper

hopper

crane car

steam whistle

smokestack

diesel switcher

head lamp

coal car

steam locomotive

cowcatcher

mailbags

porter

observation car

passenger cars

monorail

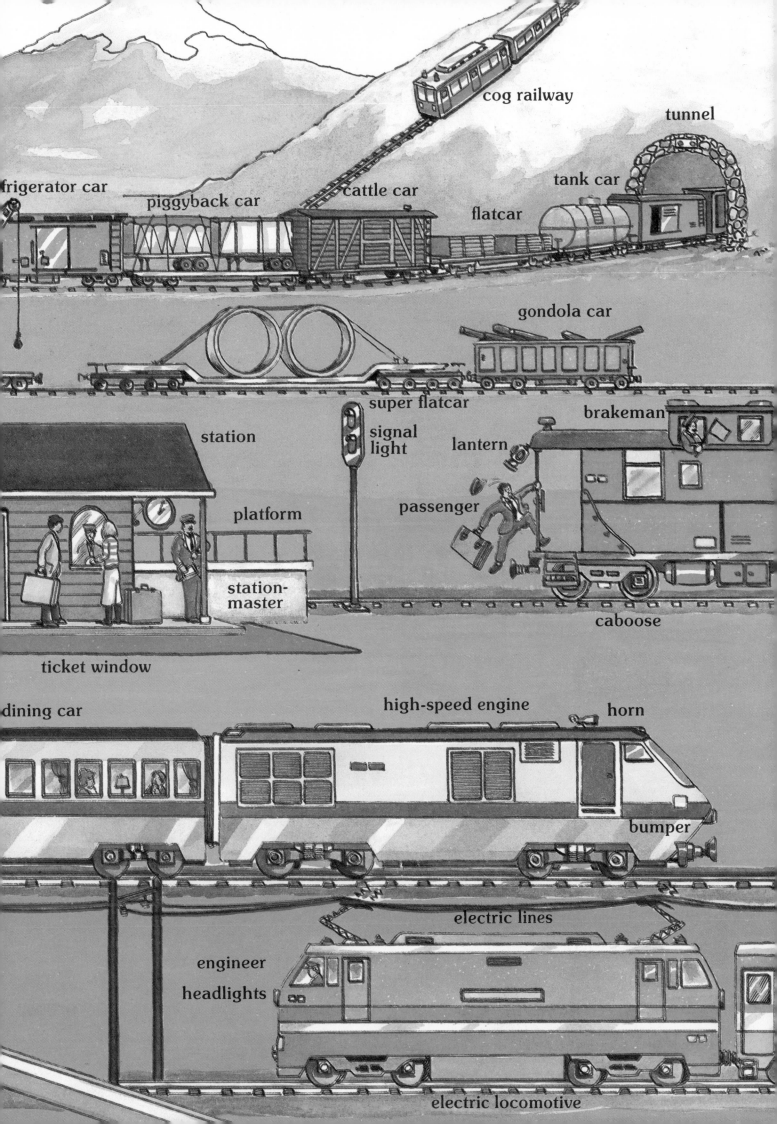

cog railway

tunnel

refrigerator car

piggyback car

cattle car

flatcar

tank car

gondola car

super flatcar

signal light

station

platform

station-master

ticket window

lantern

brakeman

passenger

caboose

dining car

high-speed engine

horn

bumper

electric lines

engineer

headlights

electric locomotive

IN THE HARBOR

container boat

lighthouse

smokestacks

life boats

cargo containers

ocean liner

bridge

ferry

hovercraft

bell buoy

speedboat

tugboat

barge

outboard motor

mast

motorboat

sport fishing boat

oars

cabin

buoy

rudder

rowboat

sloop

sailboat

bow

stern

oil tanker

anchor

periscope

sails

crow's nest

submarine

rigging

lightship

bowsprit

clipper

trawler

fishnets

loading crane

pulley

freighter

flag

flagpole

deck

freight hatches

shipping crates

fisherman

dock workers

dock

freight truck

grain sacks

rope

mooring

raft

paddle

canoe

AT A CONSTRUCTION SITE

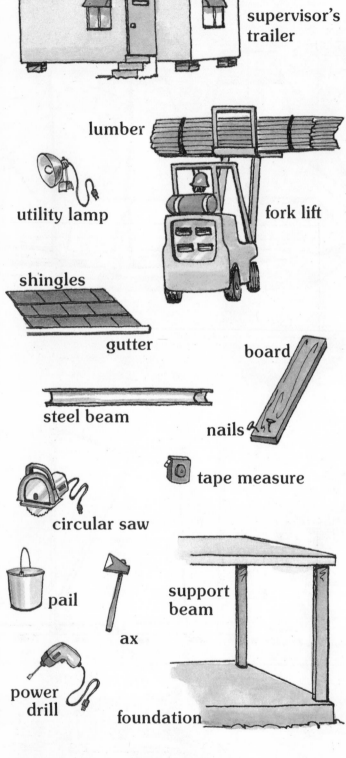

supervisor's trailer

lumber

utility lamp

fork lift

shingles

gutter

board

steel beam

nails

tape measure

circular saw

pail

support beam

ax

power drill

foundation

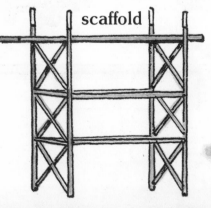

scaffold

cement trough

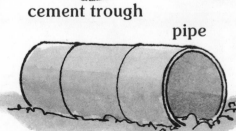

pipe

cement mixer

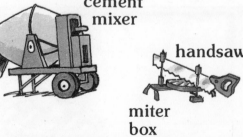

handsaw

miter box

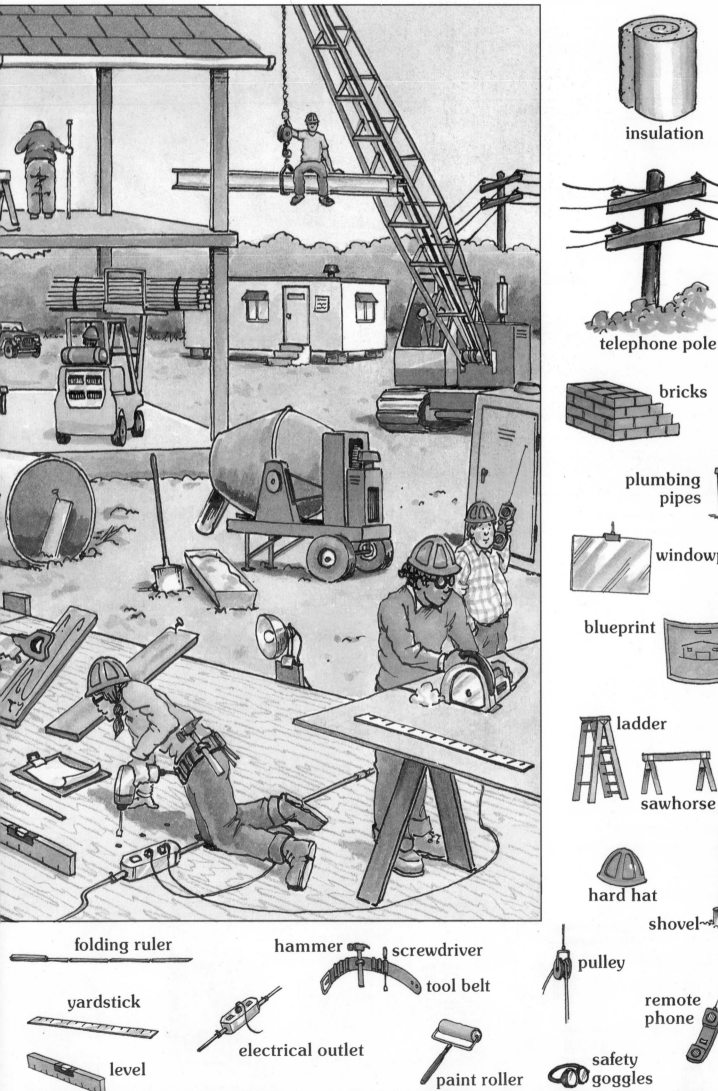

insulation

telephone pole

bricks

plumbing pipes

windowpane

blueprint

ladder

sawhorse

hard hat

shovel

folding ruler

yardstick

level

hammer   screwdriver

tool belt

electrical outlet

paint roller

pulley

remote phone

safety goggles

IN THE OFFICE

radio

pie chart

chair

typewriter

briefcase

desk

paper cup dispenser

triangle

skyline

T-square

stool

adding machine

bulletin board

bookshelf

calculator

telephone

keyboard

earphones

computer terminal

dictating machine

printer

bar graph

microphone

art supplies

envelope

clock

slide projector

slides

supply carousel

stapler

tape

calendar

photocopier

tape dispenser

package

lamp

postal scale

fire alarm

water cooler

paper clip

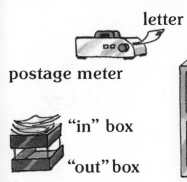
postage meter

letter

"in" box

"out" box

file cabinet

mailboxes

drafting table

paper

ON THE ROAD

moving van

bus

bucket loader

dump truck

construction worker

shovels

tank truck

detour sign

bulldozer

warning light

station wagon

steam roller

roadblock

van

water pump

tractor loader

cherry picker

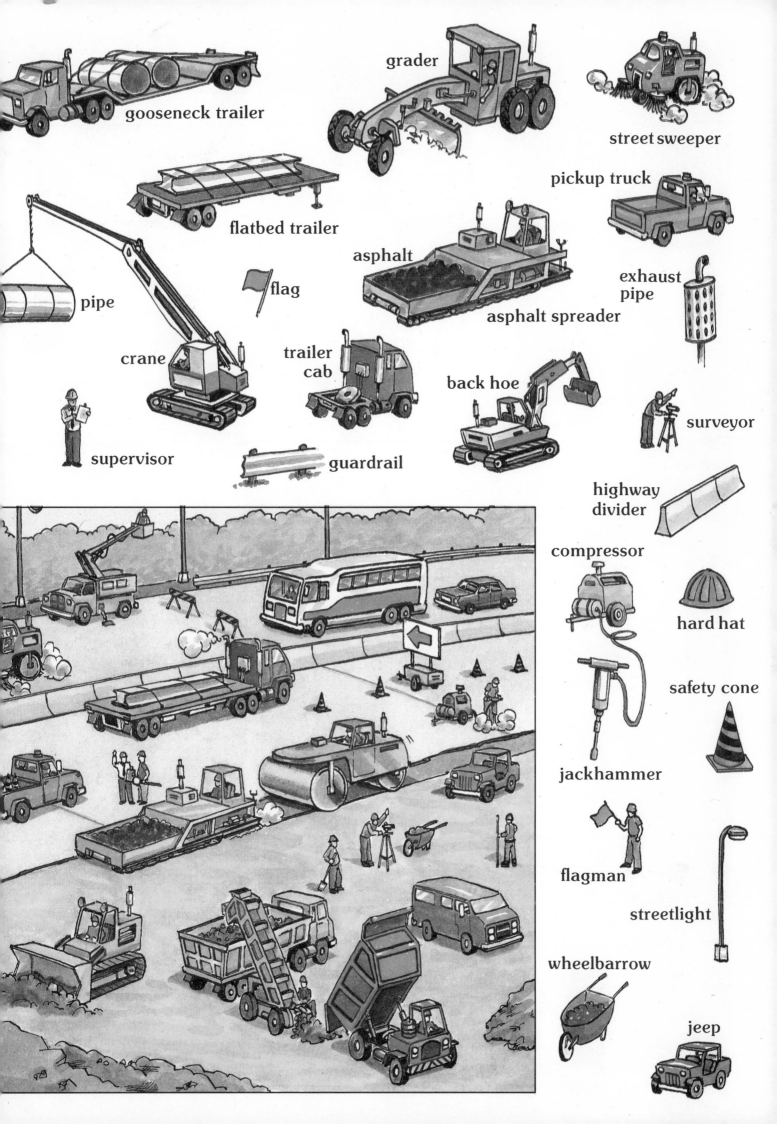

gooseneck trailer

grader

street sweeper

pickup truck

flatbed trailer

asphalt

flag

asphalt spreader

exhaust pipe

pipe

crane

trailer cab

back hoe

surveyor

supervisor

guardrail

highway divider

compressor

hard hat

safety cone

jackhammer

flagman

streetlight

wheelbarrow

jeep

WORLD AT WORK

A
adding machine
air filter
air hose
air pump
air traffic controller
ambulance
anchor
apron
art supplies
asphalt
asphalt spreader
awl
ax

B
back hoe
baggage cart
barge
bar graph
battery
bell buoy
bicycle helmet
binoculars
blimp
blueprint
board
boarding ramp
bookshelf
bow
bowsprit
brakeman
bricks
bridge
briefcase
bucket loader
building blocks
bulldozer
bulletin board
bumper
buoy
bus

C
cabin
caboose
calculator
calendar
canoe
cargo containers
cargo plane
cash register
cattle car
cement mixer
cement trough
chair
cherry picker
circular saw
clipboard
clipper
clipper ship
clock
coal car
cockpit
coffee maker
cog railway
compressor
computer terminal
construction worker
container boat
control tower
convertible
conveyor belt
covered hopper
cowcatcher
crane car
crowbar
crow's nest

D
deck
desk
detour sign
dictating machine

diesel engine
diesel switcher
dining car
dock
docking director
docking tractor
dock workers
dollhouse
dolly
double-door boxcar
drafting table
dump truck

E
earphones
electrical outlet
electric lines
electric locomotive
engine
engineer
envelope
exhaust pipe
exit sign
extension cord

F
fan
fan belts
faucet
ferry
file cabinet
fire alarm
fire truck
fisherman
fishnets
flag
flagman
flagpole
flaps
flatbed trailer
flatcar
flight attendant

WORD LIST

fluorescent light
folding ruler
fork lift
foundation
freight elevator
freighter
freight hatches
freight truck
fuel truck

G gas cap
gas pump
generator
gondola car
gooseneck trailer
grader
grain sacks
grease gun
guardrail
gutter

H hammer
handsaw
hand truck
hangars
hard hat
headlamp
headlight
headlights
helicopter
high-speed engine
highway divider
hood
hopper
horn
hot air balloon
hubcap
hydraulic lift

I "in" box
industrial vacuum cleaner
insulation

J jack
jackhammer
jack-in-the-box
jeep
jet engine
jetliner
jet walk
jumbo jet

K keyboard

L ladder
lamp
landing gear
landing pad
lantern
letter
level
lifeboats
lighthouse
lightship
loader
loading crane
luggage
luggage carrier
lumber
lunch box

M mailbags
mailboxes
mast
microphone
miter box
monorail
mooring
motorboat
motorcycle
motor oil cans
moving van
muffler

N nails
nose

O oars
observation car
ocean liner
oil spout
oil tanker
outboard motor
"out" box

P package
packing material
paddle
pail
paint roller
paper
paper clip
paper cup dispenser
paper towel dispenser
passenger
passenger cars
periscope
photocopier
pickup truck
pie chart
piggyback car
pipe
plane
platform
pliers
plumbing pipes
porter
postage meter
postal scale
power drill
pressure gauge
printer
private jet
propeller

propeller plane
public telephone
pulley

R
radar dish
radiator
radio
raft
refrigerator
refrigerator car
remote phone
restroom
rigging
roadblock marker
robot
rocking horse
rope
rotors
rowboat
rudder
runway

S
safety cone
safety goggles
safety helmet
sailboat
sails
sawhorse
scaffold
scissors
scissors loader
screwdriver
service station
   attendant
sewing machine
shingles
shipping crates
shovels
shuttle bus
signal light
skyline
slide projector
slides

sloop
smokestack
soccer ball
speedboat
sport fishing boat
sports car
spray gun
sprinkler
squeegee
stapler
station
stationmaster
station sign
station wagon
steam locomotive
steam roller
steam whistle
steel beam
stern
stool
streetlight
street sweeper
styrofoam cups
submarine
super flatcar
supervisor
supervisor's trailer
supply carousel
support beam
surveyor

T
tail
tank car
tank truck
tape
tape dispenser
tape measure
taxicab
teddy bear
telephone
telephone pole
ten speed bicycle

terminal
thread
ticket window
timecards
time clock
tire
tire changer
tool belt
torch
toy duck
toy truck
tractor loader
trailer cab
trash can
trawler
triangle
T-square
tugboat
tunnel
typewriter

U utility lamp

V
van
vending machine

W
wagon
warning light
water bottle
water cooler
water pump
welder
wheelbarrow
wheels
windowpane
windshield wipers
wind sock
wing
wrecker
wrench

Y yardstick